The Very Oldest Pear Tree

Nancy I. Sanders

illustrated by
Yas Imamura

Albert Whitman & Company
Chicago, Illinois

Wild waves of the Atlantic Ocean tossed the wooden boat
as it sailed west. Crisp sea breezes blew across the crew
working the rigging, and shivered the leaves of a little pear
tree onboard.

The tree, a sapling, was part of a cargo shipped from
England's shores in the spring of 1630. Where was the little
tree going? America.

"Ahoy there!" John Endecott greeted the ship. He was the governor in Salem, a small settlement the Puritans built in what would become known as Massachusetts.

When the Puritans had first arrived, they found forests of trees. But there were no pear trees.

"Did you bring me a pear tree?" Governor Endecott asked the captain.

"Aye," said the ship's captain. The ship had brought an entire orchard of fruit trees!

John Endecott took the little pear tree along with the other saplings back to his garden in Salem, where he tended them carefully until they were hardy enough to plant.

In 1632, Governor Endecott built a house on his new farm looking out over two rivers that opened to the sea. There were no roads or bridges yet, so he built wharves along the water's edge to dock his shallop, a small fishing boat he rowed into town.

He planted an orchard of apple and pear trees on the farmland. But he picked the little pear tree to grow right in front of the house, and he planted it in a special ceremony. He hoped the tree would live a long time.

The tree was small yet sturdy. Though young, its roots reached deep.

The tree became known as the Endecott pear tree. Year after year it grew stronger and taller. Each spring, its buds opened into delicate blossoms. Every summer, pears grew on its branches, and bushel baskets were filled during harvest in the fall.

One day in 1644, sparks blew through the orchard. A fire had started by accident.

Black clouds billowed, and flames raged until hundreds of trees in the orchard were destroyed. But the Endecott pear tree was spared.

In time, Massachusetts became one of thirteen English colonies. Salem sprouted into a busy city. Three miles away, John Endecott's descendants farmed the land where the pear tree stood. The community surrounding the farm became the town of Danvers.

As generations passed on the Endecott farm, the family changed the spelling of their name to "Endicott," and the new spelling was used for the pear tree too. After many years, old barns and stables were replaced, the wharves fell into disrepair, and Governor Endecott's house no longer stood.

But the pear tree remained, surrounded by cornfields and meadows.

In 1775, when the American Revolutionary War began and
Paul Revere made his famous midnight ride from Boston to
Lexington, the Endicott pear tree was nearly one hundred
fifty years old.

After the war, when the United States of America was born,
and Massachusetts and the other colonies became states,
the Endicott pear tree grew new branches that reached up
sturdier and stronger than ever.

George Washington was the nation's first president, followed by John Adams. After John Adams finished his term in 1801, he moved back to his farm, about a day's journey from the pear tree. One day a friend stopped by Adams's farm and left pears from the old Endicott tree and a note encouraging him to try the fruit and "eat with our forefathers."

By now the tree was a living legend.

The landscape around the pear tree was slowly changing with the Industrial Revolution. Danvers became a prosperous town in the shoemaking industry, with dozens of shoe manufacturers in the 1850s. Railroads were being built, and better roads. Travel was easier, and people came from greater distances to see the old pear tree.

Henry Wadsworth Longfellow, who lived near the tree, wrote a letter to a schoolteacher in 1879. Her students wanted to know why the seventy-two-year-old poet could write things that sounded as if he "were as happy as a boy."

He told them about the pear tree, which by then was more than two hundred years old. "I suppose the tree makes new wood every year, so that some part of it is always young," Longfellow wrote. He added, "I hope it is so with me."

As the 1800s continued and more and more forests were replaced by cities and industry, many Americans began to think about nature—and trees—in ways they hadn't before. Towns and cities across the country celebrated a new holiday called Arbor Day, holding special ceremonies to plant trees, and trees were the subject of popular songs and verses. "He who plants a tree / Plants hope," wrote a Massachusetts poet named Lucy Larcom.

The pear tree inspired Larcom too. She composed a poem honoring it for Arbor Day in 1890. "Still a growing, breathing thing— / Autumn, with the heart of spring."

The old tree was more than three hundred years old when storm clouds gathered in 1938. Wild winds whipped its branches, twisting and tearing them off. The worst hurricane in the history of New England battered the tree.

But the branches grew back.

The Endicott family sold the farm, and then the land changed hands again. By the 1950s the tree stood near a factory that made vacuum tubes for radios and television sets. Off the edge of the factory's parking lot, the tree was nearly out of sight.

Under the cover of darkness, in July of 1964, silent figures crept up to the tree.

By the time these vandals slipped back into the night, every limb had been hacked away. Only the twisted, torn trunks remained.

Tree experts hurried to help. They collected small green twigs from the chopped-off branches. Carefully peeling back the bark on the trunks, the experts inserted the twigs, sealed the grafts with wax, and wrapped each one with burlap. Yet not a single graft worked.

But the Endicott pear tree reached deep, deep down into the soil. It pulled up rich nutrients through its strong roots. Slowly, almost miraculously, a hundred tiny branches sprouted along its trunks. It survived!

Now a fence protects the pear tree, and rows of larger trees shelter it from storms. A medical center has replaced the factory.

In 1997, a cutting from the tree branches was used to grow a new Endicott pear tree. This clone, or copy of the pear tree, was planted at the National Clonal Germplasm Repository in Oregon, an important storage bank for plants and seeds. Now, instead of cutting twigs from the old tree to plant, people can use cuttings from the clone. Endicott pear trees have been planted across the nation with these cuttings.

Today, the Endicott pear tree is about four hundred years old. When John Endecott first planted it in front of his house, he expected the pear tree to outlive him by more than a hundred years. But no one imagined its story could still be told today.

The Endicott pear tree is a survivor. It's older than
our nation. And it's still standing strong.

Author's Note

While the Endicott pear tree is certainly not the first tree planted in North America—Native Americans and European settlers had planted trees before—the Endicott tree is significant for having such a long recorded history.

The Puritan settlement at Salem was originally known as Naumkeag, named after the native tribe living in that region, and John Endecott, who arrived there in 1628, was the settlement's first governor. Then in 1630, John Winthrop came on the ship *Arbella* to take over for Endecott as governor of the region, which had become known as the Massachusetts Bay Colony. Some sources say that the *Arbella*'s cargo included trees for planting, either as seeds or scions, which are living twigs taken from another tree and specially prepared for planting. Details about the beginnings of the pear tree are foggy, but in 1632, England granted Endecott property just three miles outside of Salem. He called his land Orchard Farm. It was here, in a special ceremony, that the former governor planted one pear tree in front of the governor's mansion. Endecott was known to have said, "No doubt when we have gone the tree will still be alive."

The tree was called the Governor's Tree, or the Endecott pear tree. (Often it is spelled Endicott since the family name was changed in the 1700s.) One day a terrible fire broke out and raged over the farmland. More than five hundred trees were lost, but the Endicott pear tree survived. During the 1800s, Reverend William Bentley frequently visited the Endicott family and their historic pear tree, writing about it in his diary. In September 1809, Bentley took a basket of Endicott pears to the town of Quincy. Finding former President John Adams away for dinner, Bentley left the pears along with the note, "To the man worthy to eat with our forefathers." The following year it was Bentley who delivered the scions, or "twigs," which Adams gladly planted on his farm.

Jeff Sanders

The author and the Endicott pear tree.

Historically, the tree has survived numerous hurricanes as well as incidents of vandalism and periods of neglect. Over the years it has continued to bear pears of a small, gritty, and harsh-tasting variety that are ideal for cooking jelly or pies. Today the Endicott pear tree stands near Salem in Danvers, where the people of the community, the medical center that owns the land, and the Endicott family help oversee its care. Identifying the tree is a nearby plaque, placed there in 2011 by the Gov. John Endecott chapter of the Colonial Dames.

In honor of the historic tree, in 1997 Joseph Postman took scion wood from the Endicott pear tree and grafted it onto rootstock at the National Clonal Germplasm Repository (NCGR) in Oregon. This repository is a gene bank, a collection of fruit trees, berries, and seeds that represents the world's diversity of crops. The Endicott pear tree clone has been used to propagate hundreds of Endicott pear tree descendants which have been planted around the country, primarily by Endicott family members whose love for the dear old pioneer tree continues to blossom anew in each generation.

Acknowledgments

A special thanks to the many dedicated people who have helped me with this project: Danvers historian and archivist Richard B. Trask; Joseph Postman with the National Clonal Germplasm Repository (NCGR); Marianne Peak and Kelly Cobble at the Adams National Historical Park; the staff of the Massachusetts General Hospital/North Shore Center for Outpatient Care; and Bill Endicott, President of the John Endecott Family Association. I also want to thank my wonderful editor, Wendy McClure, whose vision and passion for this project helped it blossom into its final form. A heartfelt thank-you is also given to the very talented illustrator, Yas Imamura, who helped bring this story to life. And finally, thanks to my husband, Jeff, whose feedback and assistance with research was invaluable (as always). What a great time we had traveling to Danvers to visit this brave old tree!

Find Out More

Visit www.danverslibrary.org/archive/what-a-pear to read a detailed history of the Endicott tree with photos and historical documents from the Danvers Archival Center at the Peabody Institute Library in Danvers, Massachusetts.

Visit www.nancyisanders.com/endicott-pear-tree for an educator's guide and information about ordering a clone of the Endicott tree for planting.

To one of America's newest patriots, our grandson Tyler, welcome to our family tree. With love from Grandma Nancy. "Pass the story down from generation to generation." Joel 1:3—NIS

To my Mom and Dad.—YI

Library of Congress Cataloging-in-Publication data is on file with the publisher.
Text copyright © 2020 by Nancy I. Sanders
Illustrations copyright © 2020 by Albert Whitman & Company
Illustrations by Yas Imamura
First published in the United States of America in 2020 by Albert Whitman & Company
ISBN 978-0-8075-6681-7 (hardcover)
ISBN 978-0-8075-6680-0 (ebook)

Design by Rick DeMonico

For more information about Albert Whitman & Company,
visit our website at www.albertwhitman.com.